sources

S0-DFS-313

Stanford, CA 94305

3 0050 01023 7054

CLASSIC CARS

by Robert B. Jackson

illustrated with photographs

HENRY Z. WALCK, INC. / NEW YORK

LIBRARY OF CONGRESS CATALOGING IN PUBLICATION DATA   JACKSON, ROBERT B.
CLASSIC CARS. SUMMARY: DISCUSSES LUXURIOUS, EXPENSIVE, CUSTOM-MADE
AUTOMOBILES BUILT BETWEEN 1925 AND 1942. INCLUDES THE BUGATTI, BENT-
LEY, ALFA ROMEO, DUESENBERG, CORD, STUTZ, AND OTHERS.   1. AUTOMOBILES
— HISTORY — JUVENILE LITERATURE.   [1. AUTOMOBILES — HISTORY]   I. TITLE.
TL147.J33   388.34′22′09043   73-7530   ISBN 0-8098-2094-3

Acknowledgments

THE AUTHOR WISHES TO THANK the following for their help
in preparing this book:

John W. Burgess, Sr., Director-Manager, Briggs Cun-
ningham Automotive Museum, Costa Mesa, Ca.; the Classic
Car Club of America; Dave Dennison, Press Information
Manager, Mercedes-Benz of North America, Inc.; Henry E.
Edmunds, Director Ford Archives, Henry Ford Museum,
Dearborn, Mi.; James W. Edwards, Services Supervisor,
Harrah's Automobile Collection, Reno, Nv.; J. R. Mauller,
Manager, Early American Museum, Silver Springs, Fl.;
Thomas I. H. Powel, Southport, Ct.; Joel Schointuch, Ad-
vertising Manager, Life-Like Products, Inc.; and Judith H.
Sussman, Marketing Services Coordinator, Gabriel Industries,
Inc.

Photographs are reproduced by courtesy of the following:
Briggs Cunningham Automotive Museum, pages 19, 27 and
43; Mercedes-Benz of North America, Inc., page 21; Thomas
I. H. Powel, page 29; Early American Museum, pages 32 and
49; Hubley Division, Gabriel Industries, Inc., page 38;
Harrah's Automobile Collection, page 41; Ford Archives,
page 53.

Other photographs are by the author.

Contents

1 / *Majestic Giants of the Past*

SMELLING OF LEATHER AND OIL, swift and elegant, the big luxury cars of the late twenties and thirties represent the best of fine automobiles. Majestic giants of the past like the American Duesenberg, English Bentley, French Hispano-Suiza and Italian Isotta-Fraschini now bring much higher prices than when they were new because of this excellence in combination with their scarcity.

Such cars were produced late enough in the development of the automobile to have all the basic mechanical features of current mass-produced cars. In addition, however, they were built at a time when the individuality, distinguished design and workmanship of automobiles made entirely by hand was still economically possible. Therefore these automobiles have set standards against which all other cars must be judged, and they are called "classic cars" as a result.

But "classic" is a word that has been used so widely and so loosely that it has lost some of its meaning; and it is not a particularly exact word when used to describe an automobile, anyway. For these reasons some disagreement exists among the experts as to just which cars deserve to be called classic.

The best authority is the Classic Car Club of America, an organization of some four thousand admirers and collectors who are highly dedicated to the preservation of classic cars. According to their definition a classic car must have been made between 1925 and 1942. These specific dates were chosen because by 1925 all the basic mechanical features of today's cars (such as four-wheel brakes) had been introduced, and in 1942 U.S. automobile production was stopped because of World War II. None of the cars made after the war meet the Classic Car Club of America's other standards except the Lincoln Continentals of 1946-48.

For the CCCA has also ruled that a classic car must have been a limited-production luxury automobile with special technical features, and not have been strictly mass-produced. Mass-produced cars can be turned out quickly in large numbers and sold for far less than handmade automobiles, but cars manufactured on fast-moving production lines must have many compromises made in their design and quality.

In contrast classic cars were made slowly, one at a time, with virtually no regard for time, trouble or cost. Painstakingly constructed by the most skilled craftsmen available, from the finest materials to be had, to the exacting specifications of the best designers, they were as close to perfection in every aspect as was humanly possible.

Their technically superior and very powerful engines, for instance, were assembled with the precision of a costly watch. Noted for performance, reliability and silence, they are also almost impossible to wear out. Another difference from modern engines is that they are attractive to look at, with neat, uncluttered and highly "sanitary" engine compartments and their outside surfaces either expensively enameled or polished to mirror-brightness.

A famous demonstration by an Hispano-Suiza once proved just how well such engines were put

The large but tidy aluminum straight-eight engine of a 1930 Isotta-Fraschini 8A. Each of the two carburetors supplies gasoline to four cylinders.

together. The Hisso was driven hard over 1,100 miles from Paris to Nice and back again, then immediately parked over a large sheet of white paper. Not the slightest trace of water or oil ever dropped from the engine.

Impressive as the engines of classic cars are,

though, it is the eye-catching appearance of the mighty automobiles that turns heads to this very day. Spacious and imposing in size, the majority of classic cars are even longer than most large automobiles of the present. They are also much higher and roll on big wheels (usually wire) that are twice the diameter of current models'.

In spite of this bulk most classic cars have tasteful lines and balanced proportions that are still strikingly handsome. At the front there is usually a huge, brightly chromed radiator, topped with an ornate cap and flanked by mammoth exposed headlights. On either side of an enormously long hood, spare wheels typically nestle in shallow wells located in the gracefully sweeping front fenders; and at the rear there is often a boxy leather-covered trunk or a big suitcase rack. As for body styles, the sports cars are apt to be open, two-seated, boat-tailed speedsters while the touring automobiles range from cabriolets (now called convertibles) to stiffly formal town cars in which the passengers are enclosed but the chauffeur drives in the open.

Much of the appeal of classic "coachwork" lies in its individuality. Most companies that built classic cars sold only a bare chassis for which the customer then arranged with a coachwork firm to design and build a custom body. (Some owners went so far as to order *two* bodies per chassis, an open body for summer and a closed style for winter.)

Stunning on the outside, these one-of-a-kind bodies are also lavishly trimmed on the inside. Upholstered in the most expensive fabrics and leathers, carpeted like a drawing room and inlaid with mahogany, walnut or rosewood, many also

Most classic cars have tasteful lines and balanced proportions that are still strikingly handsome. This is a 1928 Hispano-Suiza H6b town car.

have silk curtains at the windows for privacy. Having been built to order, they vary as to special fittings. There are cars with built-in luggage, picnic sets, bars and even toilets in the back seat, and some have telephones from the rear to the chauffeur up front. (The chauffeur or owner-driver had his special features, too; many classics are automatically lubricated by stepping on a special pedal, for example.)

All this luxury and mechanical perfection was extremely expensive, of course. At a time of economic depression when ordinary mass-produced automobiles sold for a few hundred dollars, the big limited-production classics cost many thousand. This meant that only a few of the richest people could afford them; and the original owners were usually millionaires, maharajahs or movie stars, many of whom bought their cars for snob appeal.

But over the years dedicated automotive enthusiasts such as members of the Classic Car Club of America have searched out the remaining examples of this glamorous machinery and carefully restored them so that all may appreciate their excellence. So great is the dedication of classic car fanciers, in fact, that one owner is said to have directed in his will that he be buried at the wheel of his beloved automobile.

2 / *Classic Cars From Abroad*

France

Bugatti (boo-gŏt-tē′). Ettore Buggatti, an Italian, built his famous cars in Molsheim, a small town in eastern France, most of them between the two World Wars. Nearly everyone in Molsheim worked for him; their food was raised locally, and Bugatti had his own hotel, museum, boatyard and distillery near the factory. He even constructed his own generating plant for electricity after the local power company offended him by sending a second-notice bill.

There were also stables in Molsheim because Bugatti was an enthusiastic horseman who often wore stylish riding clothes on his morning tours of the factory. He wanted his cars to be thoroughbreds like his horses; and their radiators were shaped like a horseshoe, perhaps to symbolize this intention.

Only "Le Patron," as Bugatti liked to be called, had the keys to his buildings; and he made every important decision in Molsheim as well as most of the minor ones. He was so egotistical that he named a daughter with his initials, "L'Ebé"; and it has been said that the haughty Bugatti once refused to sell a car to the King of Albania because he dis-

approved of the King's table manners. In addition to being a crusty individualist, Bugatti was also a self-taught mechanical genius, however; and he produced six thousand or so of the world's finest automobiles.

Bugatti not only built the most successful racing cars in Europe but fast, luxurious touring automobiles as well, noted for their cornering and road-holding ability. The best of the road "Bugs" is usually thought to be the Type 57, which had an eight-cylinder engine with two overhead camshafts and was equipped with shock absorbers costing one thousand dollars a set.

The photograph shows a 57SC Bugatti at speed. "S" means a sports version, and "C" indicates that the engine has a supercharger (*compresseur* in French) pumping additional gasoline and air mixture into the cylinders for greater power. The car was constructed in 1936 for Baron Rothschild of France and when delivered it was capable of 130 mph. Its dramatic "Atlantic" coupe body was designed by Jean Bugatti, Ettore's son, who was later killed in another Type 57 while trying to avoid a postman who had ridden his bicycle onto the Molsheim test track.

The characteristically blue body of this 57SC

is made of a special lightweight aluminum alloy that could not be welded, and the unusual flanges along the hood, roof and fenders are where the body panels have been riveted together. In 1971 the car was sold for $59,000 at a Los Angeles auction, then a record price, to a Bugatti enthusiast who already owned twelve other Bugs.

Hispano-Suiza (ēs-pŏ'-no swēs'-ă). The large and stately Hispano-Suiza received its name because it was first built in Spain from the designs of a Swiss engineer, Marc Birkigt. Birkigt, who had originally left Switzerland for Spain to work on electric locomotives, became factory manager and chief designer for the Hispano-Suiza organization at the time it was formed in Barcelona in 1904. Among the company's first successes was a very early four-cylinder sports car named "Alfonso" after the King of Spain, an enthusiastic owner who was later to buy the first car of every model that Hispano-Suiza introduced.

When World War I interrupted automobile production, Hispano-Suiza turned to the manufacture of aircraft engines. Military planes were then being used for the first time, and Birkigt designed a revolutionary lightweight V-8 aviation engine that proved to be one of the best.

The "Hisso" aircraft engine powered such famous combat planes of World War I as the British SE-5, the French Spad and the French Nieuport; and it was a favorite of French ace Georges Guynemer who mysteriously disappeared while on a mission in 1917. The emblem on the sides of the planes in his squadron was a flying stork; and when Hispano-Suiza resumed making automobiles after the war every car had a small statue of a similar stork mounted on its radiator cap.

Birkigt applied many of the technical improvements he had developed for his aircraft engine to the cars he built in the twenties. One of his greatest was the Type H6, first manufactured in both Barcelona and Paris but later produced primarily in Paris alone. The photograph shows an H6c "Boulogne," named after a race in which similar cars placed first and second in 1923.

Extremely advanced mechanically, the H6 Hispano-Suiza had an enameled six-cylinder engine with two spark plugs for each cylinder and a crankshaft that was skillfully machined instead of being cast like modern versions. From a 770-pound block of the finest steel obtainable, 671 pounds were slowly ground away to make each ninety-nine-pound crankshaft. As a result of this and other costly

manufacturing methods, Hispano-Suizas were the most expensive cars on the road in their day, priced in the vicinity of $20,000.

The largest Hispano-Suiza, the twelve-cylinder Type 68 which succeeded the H6, was built in Paris from 1931 until 1938 when the company had to concentrate on military matters once more. Despite weighing nearly five thousand pounds and having a 158-inch wheelbase in its longest version, the super-luxurious Type 68 could easily top one hundred miles an hour.

Mercedes-Benz (mēr-sâd'-ēs bĕnz). Germans Gottlieb Daimler and Karl Benz are usually given credit for building the first practical gasoline motor vehicles, Benz in 1885 and Daimler in 1886. Both automotive pioneers formed companies to manufacture cars for sale; and in 1926 these firms were combined to form Daimler-Benz. By then cars built by the Daimler company had been renamed "Mercedes" for the daughter of a financial backer; and models produced by the new organization were called Mercedes-Benz.

Both factories had been active in racing before their merger; and shortly after their combination Mercedes-Benz became known throughout Europe for its "S" series of fast white sports cars. Big and high, with long, slotted hoods and a stack of two thirty-three-inch spare wheels usually mounted at the rear, the "S" cars were supercharged for extra speed; and the moaning shriek of the supercharger over the engine's loud roar is the most memorable characteristic of an "S" during brisk acceleration.

The "S" series of the Mercedes-Benz was designed by Ferdinand Porsche, who was later to design the Volkswagen "Beetle" and the first model of the sports car bearing his name. While Daimler was still independent, Porsche had first designed a rather mild Mercedes touring car and then modified his original plan to produce the Model K Mercedes. The Model K had a six-cylinder, 381-cubic-inch engine that turned out 110 horsepower without the supercharger and 160 horsepower when the "blower" was activated by tromping the accelerator to the floor. This supercharger was so powerful that it could be used for only a few seconds at a time; otherwise it would overstress the engine.

Porsche's next step was to increase the engine size of the K Mercedes to 415 cubic inches, then lower and lighten the chassis. This variation, called

the Model S, appeared in 1927 as a full-fledged Mercedes-Benz.

The S was followed by Model SS ("Sportmodell S") which had been further lightened and modified, its engine capable of a maximum of 180 horsepower. In 1928 the SSK (*kurz* is German for "short") appeared (photo), its wheelbase having been shortened from 134 to 116 inches to make it more suitable for the popular European motor sport of hill-climbing. The last—and fastest—of the fierce "S" cars were a small number of SSKL (*leicht* means "light") all-out racers, built only for use by factory teams in competition. The SSKL's, which had holes drilled everywhere, even in their frames, for still greater lightness, had big "Elephant" super-chargers, were rated at three hundred horsepower, and could reach 130 mph.

GREAT BRITAIN

Rolls-Royce. Even those who are not car buffs can usually recognize the formal gabled radiator and winged-lady hood ornament of a Rolls-Royce; and over the years the very words "Rolls-Royce" have become synonomous with the highest possible quality to the general public. While some experts may have reservations about current models, there is no doubt whatever that a Rolls-Royce constructed during the classic period was, just as the company's slogan stated, "The Best Car In The World."

Henry Royce was a constructor of electric cranes in Manchester, England, who did not build his first car until he was almost forty; and he did so then only because he was dissatisfied with the one he had just bought. Royce's effort turned out better than any automobile then on the market, and in 1904 he began the manufacture of Rolls-Royces for sale to others. They were given the double name because they were first sold by a London car dealer, Charles Rolls. Rolls, who was a pioneer motorist, balloonist and aviator, was associated with Royce for only six years; he was killed in a flying accident in 1910.

Royce believed in concentrating on making only one model at a time; and he insisted that every detail of every car be perfect, no matter how much difficulty or expense was involved. Until 1949 Rolls-Royce built chassis only, coachwork firms adding the bodies later, usually to the specifications of each customer. The main factory was first located in Manchester, then later moved to Derby (it is now in Crewe); but Rolls-Royces were also built in Springfield, Massachusetts, between 1920 and 1931.

From the beginning Rolls-Royces (the factory thinks it quite impolite to refer to one as merely a "Rolls") have been world-famous for exceptionally smooth and quiet operation; and their model names have reflected this characteristic. The long-lived "Silver Ghost" was produced from 1907 until 1925, its successor the "Phantom I" between 1925 and 1929, and Royce's last personal design, the "Phantom II," was made from 1929 until 1935.

Many Rolls-Royce fanciers regard the Continental short-chassis version of the Phantom II (photo) as the finest Rolls-Royce ever made. Its wheelbase measured 144 inches as compared to the usual 150. Fast yet arm-chair comfortable, the Continental Phantom II has a 468-cubic-inch engine that can take the big car up to nearly one hundred miles an hour. According to one owner, the only sound louder at that speed than at idle is the wind.

Bentley. Best known of the many sports cars produced in Great Britain during the twenties are the big, high Bentleys. Usually painted a dark green, Britain's official racing color, sporting Bentleys have folding windshields, bicycle-type fenders, and hefty brake levers mounted outside their large, tublike open bodies. Bentleys are also noted for their very strong construction, Ettore Bugatti once being so unkind as to remark that Monsieur Bentley made the fastest trucks in the world.

W. O. Bentley, a designer of aircraft engines during World War I, began to build these celebrated speedsters in 1919. The first Bentleys had three-liter (183-cubic-inch), four-cylinder engines; and variations among these three-liter Bentleys can be distinguished by the background colors of their winged "B" radiator badges. Three-liter Bentleys in standard trim are known as "Blue Label" cars, while "Red Label" Speed Models are faster, having been guaranteed by the factory to do ninety mph. Swiftest of all were the limited number of "Green Label" Super Sports three-liter Bentleys, capable of one hundred mph.

The "Big Six" Bentley, added to the line in 1926, has a larger six-cylinder 402-cubic-inch engine. While the "Big Six" was originally intended as a touring chassis suitable for luxurious closed "saloon" bodies rather than open sporting coachwork, the company's lively racing interest prevailed and a "Speed Six" version appeared before long.

Bentleys made their most memorable racing mark in the famous twenty-four-hour endurance race at Le Mans, France. Three-liter cars won there in 1924 and 1927, the sturdy 1927 winner persisting through the rain in spite of a collision that had knocked out a headlight, cracked a steering connection, twisted the chassis, and bent the front axle, to list only part of the damage.

The 1928 Le Mans race was won by a 4.5-liter (268-cubic-inch) Bentley which was similar to the three-liter car but had a bigger engine. In 1929 a "Speed Six" and three 4.5 Bentleys swept Le Mans with a crushing 1-2-3-4 finish; and in 1930 a "Speed Six" won again to give Bentley four straight victories. It was also about the same time that a group of

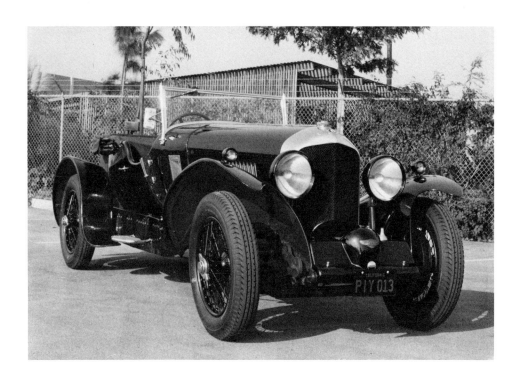

enthusiasts called the "Bentley Boys" supercharged a small number of 4.5 cars to produce the powerful "Blower Bentleys" (photo), fastest of them all.

A massive eight-liter (487-cubic-inch) touring Bentley was introduced by the factory in 1930, but only about a hundred were ever made. The worsening economic depression dealt a final blow to the company's already tottering finances; and in 1931 the Bentley organization was absorbed by Rolls-Royce.

Alfa   Romeo   (ăl-fă′   rō-mā′-ō).   A.L.F.A.
stands for Anonima Lombarda Fabbrica Automobili,
the Lombardy Automobile Manufacturing Company, formed in 1909 in Milan, capital of the Lombardy region of northern Italy. "Romeo" comes from
industrialist Nicola Romeo, who took over the company in 1915; and since its beginning Alfa Romeo
has made fine high-speed touring automobiles,
sports cars and all-out racing models.

After World War I, when the Alfa factory team
became prominent in European competition, one
of its drivers was Enzo Ferrari, now the manufacturer of prestigious Italian sports and racing cars
himself. It was Ferrari, among others, who per-
suaded another young man, Vittorio Jano, to leave
Fiat and come to Alfa, where he was to establish
his reputation as one of the foremost automotive
designers in the world.

Jano's first production Alfa was the revolutionary Tipo (type) 6C of 1925 in which he completely broke away from the then-common practice
of building large cars with big engines. The Alfa
Romeo 6C was much shorter, lighter and lower than
most other automobiles of the time because Jano
had correctly reasoned that a light, low and highly

responsive car would handle better and be easier to drive.

The smaller car did not need as large an engine as its heavier rivals, and Jano's high-revving engine for the 6C also turned out more power for its size than the Alfa's big competitors. At first the engine was only 1487 cubic centimeters (91 cubic inches) in capacity, then in 1929 it was enlarged to 1752 centimeters (107 cubic inches).

Because of the car's engine size it became

known as the 1750 Alfa, and three versions of the 1750 were available. The Turismo (touring) 1750 had a wheelbase of 122 inches and was a seventy-mph car; the Gran Turismo 1750 came in either a 114- or 108-inch wheelbase and had an eighty-mph maximum speed; while the Gran Sport, built on the short 108-inch chassis, had a super-charged engine and could do ninety-five mph. No matter their speed, however, all three variations of the 1750 would stick to the road like glue.

Most desirable of the series today is considered to be the 1750GS, with a graceful roadster body in which the driver is seated almost over the rear axle (photo). During their heyday 1750GS Alfas won nearly every race they entered; and in recognition surviving examples are usually painted blood red, the international Italian racing color.

Isotta-Fraschini (ē-sōt'-ă fräs-kēn'-ē). Italy's second great car of the classic period was also manufactured in Milan; but in contrast to the little Alfa Romeo 1750 two-seater, the Isotta-Fraschini was a big, formal limousine that was usually driven by a chauffeur. Made from 1901 until 1936 by a company started by Cesare Isotta and Vincenzo Fraschini, the splendid Isotta-Fraschini was the chief rival of the French Hispano-Suiza; and many models of the two luxury cars are quite similar in appearance. An Isotta-Fraschini can be identified by its large "IF" radiator badge; and the letters are said to stand for "Intrepida Fides" (courage and loyalty) as well as the names of the makers.

Like the Hispano-Suiza organization Isotta-Fraschini manufactured aircraft engines during World War I and applied the experience to making automobiles afterwards. Concentrating on the production of only a single model, they began building the Tipo 8 in 1919.

The imposing Tipo 8 has an eight-cylinder aluminum engine, the first "straight" (cylinders in a straight line) eight to be put into production (8A engine photo, page 10). It was also equipped with four-wheel brakes, Isotta-Fraschini having been the first automobile manufacturer to standardize their use. The Tipo 8 was a very expensive car, a bare chassis alone selling for approximately $6,500 in the United States, where more Isotta-Fraschinis were purchased than in Europe. Among Tipo 8 owners in this country were such public figures as fighter Jack Dempsey, actor Rudolph Valentino and William Randolph Hearst, the newspaper publisher.

An improved version, the Tipo 8A (photo), succeeded the 8 in 1924, and was itself replaced by the 8B in 1931. The 8B is generally thought to be the finest Isotta-Fraschini, but few were sold. Financially hard times had come with the economic crisis of the Great Depression, and there was little market for cars that were so elegant and costly. A surviving example, for instance, has polished mahogany tool boxes, trimmed in silver, mounted on its running boards. As one writer has pointed out, a buyer could get ten Buicks for the price of a single Isotta-Fraschini in the United States; and most people could not even afford a Buick.

In 1932 Henry Ford was ready to buy the struggling concern, but the Italian government did not want foreign ownership of Isotta-Fraschini and refused to allow the purchase. The declining company survived until just after World War II by increasing its manufacture of marine and aircraft engines and by making military vehicles.

3 / *U.S. Classic Cars*

Auburn. The Auburn 851 Speedster does not meet the usual high-cost requirement for being called a classic car because it was not very expensive originally. It does measure up to classic standards in terms of its performance and styling, however. In fact, an Auburn Speedster's price of $2,245 in 1935 was so low in comparison to the car's overall quality that it was one of the biggest automobile bargains ever offered.

The Auburn company, located in Auburn, Indiana, first built cars in 1900 but did not produce particularly distinguished automobiles until the colorful Errett Lobban Cord took over the organization. Cord was hired as general manager in 1924, became vice-president the following year, and was then made president in 1926.

A fast-moving salesman, promoter and organizer, E. L. Cord claimed to have made and lost $50,000 three times before he was twenty-one. Before coming to Auburn, for example, Cord had arrived in Chicago with less than fifty dollars to his name, become a car salesman, and done so well that he wound up as general manager and part owner of the automobile agency.

By the time Cord reached Indiana the Auburn company had fallen into financial trouble because

it was not selling many cars; but the hustling "boy wonder" quickly changed all that. Building more attractive cars and then advertising them heavily, Cord multiplied Auburn sales over ten times within five years.

The best Auburn that he made was the next-to-last model to be produced, the 1935 851 Speedster (photo). A long, rakish roadster sporting tear-drop fenders and a racy boat-tail, the 851 Speedster had a supercharged 280-cubic-inch engine. Four flexible chrome-plated exhaust pipes curved downward *outside* the hood on the driver's side; and, unusual for its day, there were no running boards.

Each of the approximately five hundred 851 Speedsters that were sold (all at a loss to the company) had a signed plate on the instrument panel stating that the car had been tested at speed before it left the factory and had exceeded one hundred miles an hour. Since then, however, some critics have complained that these plates were installed before the cars were ever finished.

In 1935, as part of an advertising campaign, an 851 Speedster was taken to the Bonneville Salt Flats in Utah where it set several records for stock cars. Among them was an average speed of 102.9 mph for twelve hours, and an Auburn thus became the first fully equipped U.S. stock car to exceed one hundred mph for so long a time.

Duesenberg (dōoz'-ĕn-bẽrg). Sometimes mistakenly thought of as a German car, the Duesenberg is probably the greatest automobile ever built in the United States. Fred S. Duesenberg was born in Germany, it it true, but he and his younger brother, August, came to Iowa as boys. As young men they first set up as bicycle manufacturers, then later progressed to the building of highly successful racing cars. During World War I they made military engines, including Bugatti aircraft engines under license from Molsheim.

The first Duesenberg passenger car was the Model A, manufactured in Indianapolis, Indiana, from 1921 until 1926 by Fred with Augie's assistance. The expensive Model A, made to the highest mechanical standards, was the first U.S. car to have a straight-eight engine, an overhead camshaft and hydraulic brakes. It did not sell well, however, for the Duesenbergs were not particularly good businessmen; and their company was near financial collapse by 1926.

At that point none other than the energetic E. L. Cord took over financial control of the concern, and it was decided to produce a new model. The result

was the biggest, fastest, best-looking, most advanced, most powerful and most luxurious automobile yet seen in America. Known as the Model J unsupercharged and the SJ when supercharged, it was also the most expensive U.S. car to date, the chassis alone costing as much as ten thousand depression dollars.

Built primarily between 1930 and 1936, the magnificently gigantic J-type Duesenbergs could be purchased by only the very rich. They were widely recognized as the best U.S. automobiles on the road, though; and the still-heard phrase, "It's a doozy," came into the language during the thirties to describe other things of unmatched excellence as well.

Racing Duesenbergs had won the Indianapolis 500 in 1924, 1925 and 1927; and the 420-cubic-inch straight-eight engine of the J cars was based directly on those of the racers. Because of its racing heritage an SJ Duesenberg could reach more than one hundred miles an hour in *second gear* alone and had a top speed of something like one hundred and thirty miles an hour. Each S and SJ chassis was tested for five hundred miles at the Indianapolis Speedway before it went to a U.S. or European coachwork firm for the glamorous body that could increase its price by as much as another $10,000. The photograph shows a Hubley model of a 1930 SJ.

The Duesenberg was known for the completeness of its instrument panel which even included lights that went on when it was time to change the oil and add water to the battery. In many Deusies this extensive panel was duplicated in the rear seat so the passengers could also keep track of the car's performance.

Cord. Even though he was already producing the fleet Auburns and mighty Duesenbergs in the late Twenties, Errett Lobban Cord then decided to build another car. It was to cost somewhat more than the Auburn but far less than a Duesenberg, he determined, and it would bear his own name.

/ 39

The L-29 Cord made its debut in 1929, and like Cord's other cars proved an immediate attention-getter. The sleek, low-lined L-29 used an unusual drive system. At that time, as now, the engines of most automobiles turned the rear wheels to push the cars along; but the engine of the new Cord drove the front wheels directly. This system pulled the car down the road and enabled it to corner better. Unfortunately, the stock-market crash of 1929 occurred only a few months after the introduction of the L-29, and the unconventional car sold poorly in the bleak depression that followed. The L-29 had to be withdrawn from production in 1932.

By 1934 money was so scarce that sales of Auburns and Duesenbergs had slumped to the point that Cord's automotive empire was close to bankruptcy. His characteristic solution was to risk everything on one last revolutionary model, the 810 Cord, and that gamble almost worked.

The new car created a sensation wherever it was exhibited, partly because of the front-wheel drive carried over from the L-29 but mostly because of the 810's styling that was years ahead of its time. Even as late as 1952, seventeen years later, the Museum of Modern Art in New York City chose the 810 as one of the ten best examples of industrial styling to be found. Almost shockingly modernistic for 1936, the 810 Cord had a flat, horizontally ribbed wrap-around "coffin-nose," headlights that folded back into tear-drop fenders, and such advanced details as flush-mounted taillights and a concealed gas cap.

A variation of the 810 Cord, the 812 (photo), featuring an optional supercharger, was offered for 1937; but the days of Auburn-Cord-Duesenberg were already numbered. The 810 was publicly shown before enough cars had been made to meet the demand that was aroused; and the haste to catch up on production afterwards allowed a number of 810's with faults to be sold. This mistake had a bad

effect on further sales; and, in combination with the continuing financial crisis, became the last straw for Cord's organization. Auburn-Cord-Duesenberg made its last car in 1937.

Stutz. Harry C. Stutz manufactured both racing and passenger cars in Indianapolis, Indiana, beginning in 1911. He entered the very first Stutz that was completed in the inaugural Indianapolis 500 to gain publicity; and when the brand-new automobile finished eleventh, he coined the famous Stutz slogan, "The Car That Made Good in a Day."

Best known of the early street Stutz's was a pioneer sports car called the Stutz Bearcat, first made in 1914. The popular Bearcat had big wooden wheels and a stripped chassis that carried only fenders, hooded engine and the steering wheel, plus a pair of bucket seats with the cylindrical gas tank strapped on behind. There was no body as such at all.

In 1919 Harry C. Stutz established a second organization to manufacture a new car (named HCS with his initials), selling his interest in the original company to others who continued to produce Stutz automobiles. Frederick E. Moskovics eventually became the new president of Stutz; and in 1926 the first of a series of European-style, straight-eight

Stutzes was introduced. Swift, very well made cars of progressive design, they were much lower than other U.S. automobiles of their class.

The boat-tailed speedster model, usually painted black, was called the Black Hawk; and in 1928 a Stutz Black Hawk nearly ended the Bentley domination of the Le Mans twenty-four-hour race in France. A single, privately owned Black Hawk battled a factory team of three Bentleys on their own terms, even leading the long race until dawn, but finally finished second to one of them. In this country Auburn and Stutz were arch racing rivals, and they met in 1928 at Daytona Beach to settle

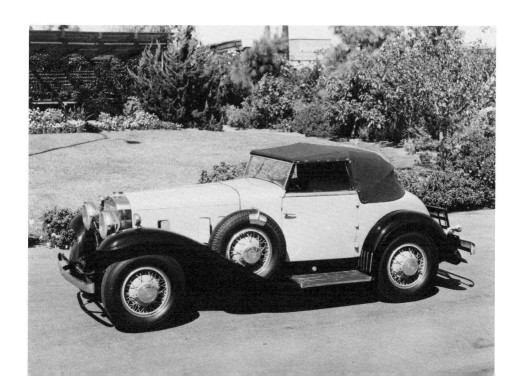

which made the faster U.S. stock car. In the confrontation on the hard-packed Florida sand, a Black Hawk averaged 106.5 mph to an Auburn Speedster's 104.3.

Later that spring the famous challenge race between a Black Hawk and an Hispano-Suiza H6c took place at the Indianapolis Speedway. Moskovics had bet $25,000 that the more agile Stutz could beat the larger Hisso "Boulogne" in a twenty-four-hour race, but lost his money when the engine of the Black Hawk failed. (The winning H6c is shown in the photograph on page 19.)

The Stutz most respected by collectors is the DV-32, built from 1931 until the company ceased operations in 1935. Its straight-eight, 322-cubic-inch engine had four valves for each cylinder instead of the usual two, "DV" standing for "Dual Valves" and "32" for their total number. There were also twin overhead camshafts to open and close the valves, another advanced feature for the time.

The "Bearcat" name was revived for sporting versions of the DV-32, which had two-seater bodies on special shortened chassis. A small number of Super Bearcats (photo) were even shorter, lighter and faster.

Packard. As Henry Royce was also to do five years later, James W. Packard decided to build his own automobile when the one he bought kept breaking down. He and his brother William completed the first Packard in 1899; and like the other cars of that time it pretty much resembled a carriage without its horse.

But unlike most other horseless carriages the one-cylinder, twelve-horsepower Model A Packard was sturdy and reliable; and after it had been put into production it sold very well. In 1901 Packard became the first U.S. car to have a steering wheel instead of the usual lever; then in 1903 the plant was moved from Warren, Ohio (where Packard had originally been a manufacturer of electrical supplies), to Detroit.

By the time James Packard retired as company president in 1909, the Packard had become a four-cylinder car. After his departure the firm continued to turn out high-quality automobiles of progressive design, introducing a six-cylinder model in 1911 which was followed, in 1915, by the "Twin Six," the first production twelve-cylinder car in the country. A Packard of that period could be recognized by the red hexagons indented in its hubcaps plus the yoke-shaped top of its radiator; and traces

of these lines could still be seen in the styling of
Packards many years later.

The basic Packard engine during the twenties
and thirties was a straight eight, handsome custom-
bodied Packard Eights being among the most prestigious cars of the day. But from 1932 (photo) until
1939 Packard also made big V-12 engines again,
and the beautiful giants with these large power
plants have become the most prized Packards of all.

Enthusiasts have often argued the merits of
these large Packards as compared to those of the

more costly European classics. Even if the edge in craftmanship *is* given to the Europeans, it must be remembered that the Packard was basically a mass-produced automobile, 5,744 Packard Twelves being made as compared to only thirty 8B Isotta-Fraschinis, for example. And, after all, it was a great accomplishment for the quality of a far less expensive, essentially production-line car to approach that of a hand-built special. In any case experts consider the Packard Eights and Twelves of the twenties and thirties to meet all the other requirements for being classics and make an exception of their origin.

In 1935 Packard started making a much smaller and cheaper automobile in an attempt to survive the depression, and the company limped along building conventional cars until 1958 when it finally collapsed. It is the classic models that Packard fanciers prefer to remember, however, for they were the cars that deserved the company's famous slogan (said to originate when someone wrote James Packard for a sales pamphlet), "Ask the Man Who Owns One."

Cadillac. While today's Cadillacs are large and luxurious in comparison to most other automobiles, time and circumstances have diminished the reputation earned by the classic Cadillacs of the thirties. Status symbol that the modern Caddie is, those who admire classic cars do not consider it to be the equal of its older relative in quality, engineering or appearance.

The earliest Cadillacs, first built in 1902, were tiny automobiles with one-cylinder engines that were manufactured by Henry M. Leland, a former machine-tool maker. They were named after Antoine de la Mothe Cadillac, the French governor of the territory of Louisiana who established Detroit, where Cadillacs have always been built, in 1701.

Leland, who became general manager of Cadillac in 1904, was one of the first to build cars from standard interchangeable parts instead of the hand-fitted individually sized pieces used previously. In 1908 his company won the English Dewar Trophy for a demonstration in which three Cadillacs were completely stripped, the parts shuffled, and then put back together again. Each of the three scrambled cars then completed five hundred miles around a race track with no trouble.

Leland's firm was taken over by the growing giant of General Motors the following year, and in 1913 the reorganized company won the Dewar

Trophy again, this time for building the first car to have an electric self-starter instead of a dangerous hand crank. Cadillacs were also the first cars to have electric lights as well as the first in the United States to have production V-8 engines.

In 1917 Henry Leland and his son, Wilfred, left Cadillac to build aircraft engines and later began work on another luxury car, the Lincoln. The Cadillac division of General Motors made great progress in spite of their loss, however, and produced its most memorable cars in the early thirties. During the classic period there were three series of Cadillacs manufactured, those with a V-8 engine, those with a larger V-12, and the fabulously complicated, gas-guzzling V-16-powered cars.

The mammoth V-16 Cadillac engine was basically two straight eights mounted at a forty-five-degree angle on a common crankcase. Each bank of eight cylinders had its own fuel pump, carburetor, water pump and ignition system, and could be operated independently. Still, in spite of its complexity, the 165-horsepower V-16 was so quiet in operation that the only sound heard at idle was the snap of electrical sparks. Just as strong as it was silent, the V-16 Cadillac engine was able to smoothly accelerate a three-ton car in high gear from a speed as low as just over two miles an hour to nearly one hundred.

V-16 Cadillacs were in production from 1930 (photo) until 1940, and fifteen fashionable body styles were generally available. As compared to a V-8 Cadillac's price of about $3,000 a V-16 could cost as much as $10,000.

Lincoln Continental. When Henry Leland and his son Wilfred left Cadillac to set up their own company in 1917, they first manufactured engines for the military aircraft of World War I. It was 1920 before they were able to produce their first automobile, which Henry Leland named for Abraham Lincoln.

The Leland Lincolns were big and costly cars of high quality; and in accordance with Henry's many posted signs of "Craftsmanship a Creed, Accuracy a Law," they were constructed with the greatest precision. Their body styling was so boxily unattractive, however, that sales were slow; and before long the firm was badly in the red. Then in 1922 Henry Ford bought the struggling concern and made it a division of his company.

Henry's son, Edsel Ford, was president of the Ford Motor Company by then and under his direction the quality of the Lincoln was strictly maintained. In addition the car's appearance and performance were much improved, and sales quickly increased. Because they were so well made and so reliable Lincolns were owned by U.S. Presidents of the time; and because of their speed they were also the favorite of gangsters and pursuing police alike during the Prohibition years.

When the depression of the thirties caused the demand for the expensive Lincolns to shrink, a medium-priced model, the Lincoln Zephyr, was placed on the market. One of the first U.S. production cars to have its frame and body built as a single unit, the 1936 V-12 Lincoln Zephyr was also the first U.S. car to be successfully streamlined.

Edsel Ford, whose primary interest was automotive styling, had the Lincoln design department work out a special convertible coupe for him in 1938 that was based on a Zephyr chassis. He had just returned from a vacation in Europe at the time, and he told his designers that he wanted the car to look "strictly continental." A particular feature upon which he insisted, even though others disagreed at first, was the car's rear-mounted, exposed spare wheel. His idea eventually proved to be one of the strongest elements of the final design.

While Edsel's "special" was not unusual mechanically, its European-style lines were so appealing that the car (photo) caused great excitement wherever he went; and many people wanted to order a duplicate as soon as they saw it. Consequently the Continental was put into limited production for the 1940 model year in both convertible and hardtop coupe forms.

But manufacture of the Continental had to be suspended in 1942 because of World War II. And then, even though production was resumed after

the war, the car's future was still in doubt because
of the increasingly expensive hand work involved.
Unable to be mass-produced, the Lincoln Continental was eventually dropped in 1948 after only
six years of life. Although the Ford Motor Company
has used the name again since then, experts favor
the original Continental and consider it to be "the
last of the classics."

CAR	BUILT	WHEELBASE IN INCHES	CHASSIS WEIGHT IN POUNDS
Bugatti 57SC	1936–38 France	117	2,100
Hispano-Suiza H6	1928–31 France	133	2,500
Mercedes-Benz SSKL	1931–33 Germany	116	2,250
Rolls-Royce Continental Phantom II	1932–35 Great Britain	144	3,750
4.5 Blower Bentley	1927–31 Great Britain	130	2,800
Alfa Romeo 1750GS	1929–34 Italy	108	2,000 with body
Issotta-Fraschini 8B	1931–36 Italy	134 or 145	3,750
Auburn 851 Speedster	1935 U.S.	127	3,700 with body
Duesenberg SJ	1932–37 U.S.	143	5,200 with body
Cord 812	1937 U.S.	125	3,500 with body
Stutz DV-32 Bearcat	1931–35 U.S.	135	4,895 with body
Packard V-12	1932–39 U.S.	139 or 144	6,000 with body
Cadillac V-16	1930–40 U.S.	148	6,000 with body
Lincoln Continental	1940–42, 1946–48 U.S.	125	3,890 with body

For comparison:

CAR	BUILT	WHEELBASE IN INCHES	CHASSIS WEIGHT IN POUNDS
Chevrolet Impala	1973 U.S.	122	4,435 with body

CYLINDERS	SIZE OF ENGINE IN CUBIC INCHES	HORSE-POWER	APPROXIMATE TOP SPEED IN MILES PER HOUR
Straight 8	199 supercharged	200	130
Straight 6	480	200	100
Straight 6	428 supercharged	300	130
Straight 6	468	company does not release	100
Straight 4	268 supercharged	240	125
Straight 6	107 supercharged	85	95
Straight 8	450	150	90
Straight 8	280 supercharged	150	104
Straight 8	420 supercharged	320	130
V-8	289 supercharged	195	110
Straight 8	322	156	105
V-12	473	175	85
V-16	452	165	100
V-12	292	120	90

V-8	350	145	95

4 / *Seeing Classic Cars*

CLASSIC CARS, rare to begin with because so few were made, have become even scarcer over the years, a number having disappeared with the passage of time. Collectors have searched out as many as possible, meticulously restoring them to showroom condition; but by now the chances of finding further unknown examples are quite slim. The days when an Isotta-Fraschini could be turned up in a forgotten corner of a junkyard or an abandoned Cord found in an old garage are just about gone at this point.

And while the total number of classic cars still in existence is relatively small (ten thousand or so in the U.S. according to the CCCA), interest in them has increased greatly recently. Thus the few classics that do change hands from time to time are sold for ever-increasing amounts; and prices have become so high that even the rich original owners of the automobiles might be shocked.

Because they are so rare and so expensive, classic cars are not apt to be seen in the parking lot of your neighborhood supermarket. There have been a few attempts at building modern replicas of classic coachwork on present-day chassis, such as plastic-bodied Cords and Auburns and the Excalibur SS which is an imitation Mercedes SSK; and you may spot one of these "replicars" on the road occasionally, it is true. They are not to be confused with the real thing, though, which are best seen in museums or at special outdoor shows.

A number of automotive museums have now been established in the United States, most of them specializing in older antique cars; but several exhibit classic cars as well. Largest of all is Harrah's Automobile Collection in Reno, Nevada, which displays over one thousand cars at a time. Among their many classics are no less than seventeen Rolls-Royces and two dozen Stutzes, for instance.

Much smaller, but a most distinguished collection, particularly of foreign classics, is the Briggs

Cunningham Automotive Museum, 250 Baker Street, Costa Mesa, California. Included in the classics there are a rare SSJ Duesenberg and the H6c Hispano-Suiza that beat the Stutz at Indianapolis.

Other good museums that feature classic cars are the Museum of Automobiles, Route 3, Morrilton, Arkansas; the Frederick C. Crawford Auto-Aviation Museum, 10825 East Boulevard, Cleveland, Ohio; and the Early American Museum in Silver Springs, Florida.

Many smaller museums are scattered throughout the country, too, not to mention numerous private collections that are often open to the public. Then there are the many individual owners of classic cars who periodically meet for outdoor competitions (frequently in association with antique car owners) during which their automobiles are judged for the beauty and authenticity of their restoration.

With the exception of CCCA events the public is usually admitted to these meetings, and attending one is just about the best way of getting a close-up look at some of these marvelous old cars. Local librarians can help find out when such shows are scheduled in your area. One good source is the

Many outdoor exhibitions of classic cars are held each year, usually in association with antique automobile meets. The light-colored car is a 1924 H6 Hispano-Suiza.

"Collectors' Calendar" in a newspaper called *Autoweek*. Even more complete listings can be found in *Hemmings Motor News* and *Old Cars*, but these newspapers are usually harder to locate.

Whenever you do have a chance to see classic cars, keep their rarity and value in mind. The basic rule for classic car watching is always: Don't Touch! Owners are nearly always pleased to answer questions about their vehicles—some even give rides at outdoor shows—but they most definitely do not appreciate finger marks, pressure on body panels

The basic rule for classic car watching is always: Don't Touch!

to see how strong they are, or anything else of the sort.

If you are not able to visit a museum or go to a show, another way of learning a great deal about classic cars is to build some of the excellent model kits that are now widely available, gradually assembling your own miniature museum. Monogram Models, for instance, has a good series of classic cars in 1/24 scale, including a 1931 Rolls-Royce Phantom II, a 1934 Duesenberg SJ, a 1937 Cord 812 and a 1941 Lincoln Continental. Monogram kits consist of plastic parts to be glued together, and they do not require painting (except for such details as door handles and taillights) if you like their choice of color. They cost about $3.50 each.

Johan Models makes a 1931 V-16 Cadillac in 1/25 scale which goes together in a similar way, although there are more parts for greater detail. There is a choice of three different body styles at around two dollars or so. As with the Monogram kits painting is not absolutely required, but if carefully done it will improve the looks of your Cadillac considerably.

The 1/25-scale classic car kits of Life-Like Products, Inc., relatively simple to build and priced at about two dollars each, are good projects for beginning modelers to try. Life-Like currently lists a Lincoln-Continental, an 812 Cord and an Auburn Speedster, and it is likely that other cars will be added to the series in the future.

Larger, more detailed and more expensive than any of the preceding are the Hubley kits. They contain as many as one hundred and fifty parts, most of them metal, which require the filing away of considerable scrap as well as painting. Beautiful models for more experienced builders, a 1/18 SJ Duesenberg (choice of two body styles) sells for about twelve dollars (see photo, page 38) and a 1/22 1930 Packard (three body styles available) is around eight dollars.

Even bigger and more detailed is the 1/12 scale Model Products Blower Bentley. This kit, which sells for about ten dollars, consists of more than 275 plastic parts, many of them plated. When completed the handsome and highly accurate model is almost fifteen inches long and only painting of a few small details is strictly necessary.

By far the most complex, most difficult and most expensive of all the classic car kits is — fittingly enough — a 1/8 scale Rolls-Royce Phantom II coupe from the Pocher company in Italy. The ultimate kit, it contains over two thousand separate pieces, most

The chassis of Model Products' highly detailed 4.5 Blower Bentley. The kit contains more than 275 parts and the finished car is almost fifteen inches long. Note the supercharger in front of the radiator.

of which are to be assembled with tiny bolts and nuts; and when completed the model's engine, steering, suspension and brakes all work like the real thing. The local hobby shop may not have one though, for availability is very limited. Then, too, there is the matter of price—the kit lists at $189.50, and assembled the model costs a staggering $985.50!